HOUGHTON MIFFLIN

Reading

A Legacy of Literacy

Voices
of the
Revolution

 HOUGHTON MIFFLIN   BOSTON • MORRIS PLAINS, NJ

California • Colorado • Georgia • Illinois • New Jersey • Texas

Design, Art Management and Page Production: Kirchoff/Wohlberg, Inc.

ILLUSTRATION CREDITS
4-25 Andrew J. Wheatcroft. **26-47** Tyrone Geter. **48-54, 56-62, 65, 67-69**
Ron Himler.

Printed in U.S.A.

ISBN: 0-618-04409-4

456789-VH-05 04 03 02 01

Voices of the Revolution

Contents

Bunker's Cove

by David Neufeld
illustrated by
Andrew J. Wheatcroff

Strategy Focus

Jack Bunker was a sailor during the American
Revolution. As you read, **evaluate** how the
author presents him and his actions.

An "old salt" is a sailor who has spent years and years at sea. Back in 1773, New England was full of old salts.

Jack Bunker was one of them. He wasn't exactly old, but he was plenty salty. He'd spent so much time in boats that his feet felt unsteady on dry land.

Jack lived on Cranberry Island, a speck of land off the coast of Maine. His sister and her husband lived nearby. Comfort and John had a farm on Norwood's Cove, a rugged and beautiful place with mountains that rose almost straight up from the water.

Life in Maine was pleasant and peaceful.
But life was not so pleasant and peaceful elsewhere
in the New England colonies. The Patriots were
growing hungry for freedom from British rule.

Right around Jack's thirty-first birthday, Massachusetts Patriots threw their famous Boston Tea Party, dumping 342 chests of tea into Boston Harbor. The tea was from the East India Company, the only company the British allowed to import tea to the colonies. By dumping it, the colonists were telling Britain they wanted freedom to make their own choices, both in matters small (what sort of tea to drink) and large (what laws to live by).

In those days, news traveled so slowly that people in Maine didn't hear about the Boston Tea Party until a year later. Even then, they didn't get too excited. ("Those wild city folk!" they said.) But by 1776 the American Revolution was in full force. British soldiers and ships were sent to rule the unruly Americans.

Meanwhile, on Norwood's Cove, John and Comfort's farm prospered.

Then one day the British ships and soldiers came. While John and Comfort were away from their farm, the British killed the family's cows and burned their house. They left a note that said, "Starve!" When John and Comfort returned, their once thriving farm was gone.

When Jack found out about this, he got mad. Mad enough to do something crazy. He and a friend set out from Norwood's Cove in a canoe. For days and days, they paddled across bays and carried their canoe across land.

Finally, they reached the Sheepscot River in Wiscassett, Maine. There they found what they'd been looking for. A British supply boat called the *Falmouth Packet*, all sixty-plus feet of it, lay peacefully at anchor. It was full of food for British troops.

Not a single British sailor was on board. They were all on shore, enjoying a nap on solid ground. So Jack and his buddy climbed aboard. They raised the sails. And off they went.

The captain of the boat opened one eye and saw his boat sailing away without him. That snapped him wide awake.

Jack and his friend gave him a wave. They laughed and sang silly sailor songs as the boat went out to sea.

Not just anyone could laugh and sing while sailing a boat like the *Falmouth Packet*.

But after a lifetime of sailing, Jack knew just how to handle the *Packet*. That's what makes a salt a salt.

The next day, Jack sailed the *Falmouth Packet* into Norwood's Cove. A boat full of supplies was a welcome sight to his sister's family. Food had been scarce since the British raid.

Jack quickly gave out the supplies. But he didn't stick around for the feast. "The British will come looking for us," he told his sister. "We don't want to be found here."

A few more men, hungry for adventure, volunteered to join him when he sailed the *Packet* back out to sea.

British warships were everywhere. It wasn't long before a British sailor looked through his spyglass and saw Jack at the wheel of the *Packet*. No British captain sailed without his uniform. Jack clearly was not a British captain. The chase began.

The British warship was armed with a cannon. If it got within shooting distance, Jack's boat would soon look like Swiss cheese.

Some boats are just built to be faster than other boats. Warships are faster than supply boats. Lucky for Jack, though, a fast boat isn't all that counts in a chase. The captain's skill counts even more.

As a heavy fog began to roll in, Jack sailed by his wits. "Keep a sharp eye on the water!" he yelled to his crew.

"Rocks dead ahead!" hollered one of the men.

Jack steered the *Packet* around them. It slipped by like a ghost.

When the fog lifted, the British were still in sight. But they didn't dare go the way Jack had gone. They crept slowly along the outside edges of the rocks.

With the British lagging behind, Jack reached his favorite hiding place on the Maine coast. It was a little cove between Great Spruce and Little Spruce Islands. The entrance was nearly invisible. Sailing into the cove was like vanishing under a magician's cloak.

Jack slipped the boat into the cove. The British weren't close enough to see where it had disappeared.

"Cut the masts!" Jack yelled. His crew got out their axes. The masts from the *Packet* crashed down into the trees on Great Spruce Island.

The British captain saw the masts before they fell. He began to steer toward the cove. But when he reached the narrow entrance, he decided it was too dangerous to risk. "Steer clear!" he shouted to his crew.

The warship sailed around to the other side of
the Spruce Islands. Still fearful of running aground
on the rocky coast, the British captain launched a
rowboat and went through a narrow channel toward
the cove where Jack and the *Packet* lay. By the time he
finally reached the cove, he found nothing. Was Jack
Bunker a magician?

No, but Jack and his friends were fast and clever.
While the British warship crawled carefully along the
coast, they had sailed the *Packet* toward land. Jack
grabbed an axe and chopped a hole in the bottom of
the boat. It sank deep into the mud.

The crew covered the *Packet* with spruce
branches. They pulled seaweed from the shore and
threw it over the parts of the boat that were showing.
They didn't want the British to get any part of the
boat. Not a single plank.

Jack and his men jumped in two rowboats and rowed to the other end of the cove. There they found another opening to the sea and escaped. They rowed by night and hid during the day. They all reached home safely.

Jack Bunker and his friends helped the Patriots fight the British until the United States won its independence. And Jack continued to sail long after that. He lived to be a *really* old salt. That little cove where the *Falmouth Packet* lay hidden became known as Bunker's Cove. And that's its name to this day.

Responding

Think About the Selection

1. What mistake does the captain of the *Falmouth Packet* make?

2. How does Jack feel after he and his friend take the *Falmouth Packet* out to sea?

3. What is the author's opinion of the British sailors who chase Jack's boat?

Author's Opinions

Copy the web on a piece of paper. Complete it with words that show the author's opinion about Jack.

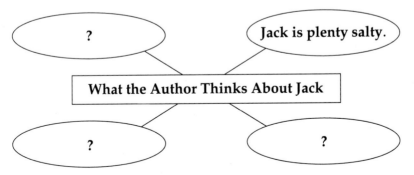

```
      ( ? )              ( Jack is plenty salty. )
          \              /
    [ What the Author Thinks About Jack ]
          /              \
      ( ? )              ( ? )
```

The DRUMMER BOY

by Philemon Sturges
illustrated by Tyrone Geter

Strategy Focus

Why do Eliza and John make friends with the enemy? As you read the story, stop now and then to **summarize** what has happened.

IT WAS 1776. Eliza Potter lived on Ferry Point Farm in Bristol, Rhode Island. She lived with her mother, her older brother, John, and her uncle, Captain Simon Potter. She helped tend geese, grow onions, and make sails for boats.

Eliza liked her chores. But most of all, she liked to sit on Seal Rock. She loved to watch ospreys dive into the sparkling water. She often saw a boy sailing a model boat on the opposite shore, and they waved to each other.

A few times each year, Eliza and John loaded a boat with onions. Then they rowed down to Newport Harbor to sell them. "Everyone loves our Bristol onions," said John. "That's mighty good for us!"

Newport had one of the very best harbors in the Colonies. It was filled with tall ships. John loved the tall ships. He was a good carpenter, and he often helped to repair them.

Thomas Strand lived just across the water from Eliza and John. His father was the commander of the British soldiers in Newport. Thomas was the drummer boy in his father's regiment.

Thomas liked living in the British army camp. And he enjoyed marching to the beat of his own drum. But most of all he liked making model boats. Back home in England, his model boats had won prizes. Thomas still sailed one of his boats when he had free time. It usually caught a brisk southwest wind and sped toward Seal Rock on the opposite shore. Sometimes he saw a girl sitting on Seal Rock, and they waved to each other.

Thomas and his father often rowed over to Bristol to have a look around. Thomas hoped to meet the girl who waved, but he never did.

Like Newport Harbor, Bristol Harbor was full of tall ships. "The ones over there belong to Captain Simon Potter, the Patriot leader," said Thomas's father. "I'm sure that he and his men are planning something. They say you can't trust those Patriots."

"Is that why we're here in the Colonies, because we can't trust the Patriots?" Thomas asked.

"In a way," said his father. "We're keeping order in the Colonies, and we have our hands full. The Patriots don't like being told what to do by King George. I won't be surprised if soon there is a war between Britain and the Patriots."

Thomas's father was right. In July 1776, the British and the Patriots went to war. In August, British ships sneaked into Bristol Harbor. They burned down Captain Potter's ships, a church, and several houses.

But the Patriots had spirit and energy. They were not discouraged. Soon Captain Potter began to build a new ship. John and Eliza had to help their uncle. John did some of the carpentry. Eliza and her mother sewed the sails. It was very hard work. When they complained a bit to their mother, she said, "It's for the cause of liberty."

Meanwhile, back in Newport at the British army camp, Thomas's father was getting ready to march. He said to Thomas, "King George has ordered us to destroy any ships that Captain Potter is building. And our spies tell us that he is building one near Bristol Harbor. We've got to hurry!"

Thomas put on his bright red uniform. His drum rolled smartly as he and his father led the soldiers to Newport Harbor. There they boarded a twenty-gun ship and sailed off toward Bristol.

The soldiers landed just north of Bristol Harbor. With Thomas in front, the soldiers marched toward the boatyard in which Captain Potter's ship was being built. As he drummed, Thomas admired the bright red coats all around him.

Now I know why the Patriots call us Lobsterbacks, he thought. Thinking about lobsters made Thomas hungry. He was tired too. It was a long, long march.

At the Potter boatyard, all of the carpenters were busy. Eliza and her mother had gone home to make lunch for the hungry crew.

Suddenly someone cried out, "The Lobsterbacks are coming!" But it was too late. When John looked over the side of the unfinished boat, he saw British soldiers coming his way. They were led by a drummer boy about his own age.

The soldiers captured John and his shipbuilding friends. They set the ship and the boatyard on fire. Then they began marching their prisoners back toward the British ship north of Bristol Harbor.

For Thomas, the march back to the British ship seemed much longer than the march toward the Potter boatyard. He had long since passed from hungry and tired to thirsty, hot, and exhausted. No one seemed to notice that his drumming had stopped and he was falling behind.

John was more angry and frightened than tired. He felt a bit better when he realized that the soldiers were headed in the direction of his home, Ferry Point Farm.

When the soldiers and their prisoners got to Ferry Point Farm, Eliza and her mother were standing next to the barn. The soldiers were so tired that they decided to rest there for a while. The commander told Eliza and her mother to bring water for the soldiers. At first Eliza and her mother didn't want to help the soldiers in any way. But then a young Lobsterback boy fainted right in front of them. Eliza ran to get him some tea and some bread with honey.

Thomas's father bent down to see what had happened to his son.

When Thomas opened his eyes, he saw his father and then Eliza. They recognized each other from all the times they had waved across the water.

First Thomas ate a bit and had a sip of tea. Then he said to Eliza, "Thank you. I hope no one has been hurt. I meant no harm to anyone. If fact, when the war stops, I want to stay in Bristol and work on boats."

"I wish my brother was here to talk to you," said Eliza. "He's a skilled carpenter and he works on boats."

43

"I *am* here," said John, to his sister's surprise. "But I've been taken prisoner."

"Why have you taken my son?" John's mother asked Thomas's father.

"It was King George's order," he answered.

"Well, I'm sure King George would be pleased that we have taken care of *your* son," said Eliza hopefully. "I know he would want to reward us by setting my brother free."

"I'm not sure about King George, but I will release your brother," said Thomas's father.

Later that day, John and Eliza gave Thomas a ride home in their rowboat. He was too tired to march back to the ship.

"Thank you," said Thomas to John and Eliza. "When the war is over, John, I will come back and learn shipbuilding from you."

"I'd like that," said John.

"Me too," said Eliza.

Thomas did indeed move to Bristol after the American Revolution. His children and grandchildren built some of the fastest boats the world has ever seen.

Responding

Think About the Selection

1. What are two of Eliza's jobs?

2. What causes Thomas to faint?

3. Why do you think Thomas's father sets John free?

Why It Happened

Copy this chart on a piece of paper. Read what happened—the effect. Think about why it happened. Write the cause.

Story Page	Cause	Effect
35	The British and the Patriots are at war.	The British burn Captain Potter's ships, some houses, and a church.
41	?	Eliza runs to get tea, bread, and honey.
45	?	John and Eliza row Thomas back to his ship.

Deborah Sampson

Soldier of the Revolution

by Lee S. Justice
illustrated by Ron Himler

Strategy Focus

Is freedom for everyone? As you read this story, think of other **questions** for discussion.

$\mathcal{D}$eborah Sampson was born in Plympton, Massachusetts, in 1760. Throughout her childhood, she heard about Boston's Patriots, also called the Sons of Liberty. She heard the talk of independence — of breaking free of Britain.

Freedom was a dangerous and exciting idea. But there was little freedom in Deborah's own life. As she later said, "I was born to be unfortunate."

When she was very young, Deborah's father sailed off on a ship and never came back. Her mother did not have enough money for food. So she decided to look for a family to take her daughter.

Often, poor parents "bound out" a child to another family. In return for a home, food, and clothing, the child would serve the family until age eighteen. Ten-year-old Deborah became a bound servant in the home of the Thomas family of Middleborough.

The Thomases treated Deborah like a daughter. Of course, sons and daughters were expected to work. Mrs. Thomas told Deborah what she should do each day.

First, Deborah had to get up at dawn to begin her household chores. Then, she must help make breakfast for the family. Next, she should feed the chickens and milk the cow. Then, she should water the vegetable garden. After that, she could sew, spin, or weave. Like all farm women, Deborah worked hard.

With the ten Thomas sons, Deborah also hunted and fished. She chopped wood and gathered hay. She did all kinds of heavy work.

Farmer Thomas didn't believe in schooling for girls. But Deborah had always been eager to learn. She already knew how to read and write.

Deborah read all the pamphlets and newspapers she could find. A minister gave her a religious book. She soon knew it by heart. She kept a journal. In it, she listed her good actions and her bad ones. She wanted to improve herself.

"I wish you wouldn't spend so much time scribbling," Farmer Thomas complained. But he did not make her stop. So Deborah continued.

At church one day, someone read an important document to the crowd. The document said, "All men are created equal." It said that people had rights — "life, liberty, and the pursuit of happiness." It listed the reasons for breaking free of Britain. At the end of the reading, the listeners leaped up and cheered.

The Declaration of Independence made Deborah's heart pound. But she wondered what some of it meant. She wondered about words like *liberty*.

The soldiers were fighting for liberty. The older Thomas boys had already left home and signed up. Was liberty only for a nation? Or could there be liberty for a sixteen-year-old farm girl?

When she turned eighteen, Deborah began working in people's homes as a weaver. She also taught children for two summers. But by the time she was twenty-one, she was eager for a change.

Deborah had an active mind. She was quiet, but in a strong, confident way. Deborah looked strong, too. And she had grown taller than other women of the time. In fact, she was taller than many men.

But while men her age had a chance to see the world and taste freedom, women didn't. Deborah decided she wanted adventure, too.

One day Deborah's Middleborough neighbors saw her going about her business as usual. The next morning she was gone.

Days later, a young man in farmer's clothes stood before an army recruiter in Bellingham, Massachusetts. "Your age?" asked the recruiter.

"Eighteen," said the young man. His face did not even have a whisker. He looked fifteen, even younger. But the army needed soldiers — young or old. The recruiter did not care.

The young farmer promised to serve for a term of three years. He signed his name: *Robert Shurtlieff.*

Robert Shurtlieff was not a teenage boy. He was Deborah Sampson in disguise.

It was 1782. Fifty recruits hiked west through the Berkshire hills. Hour after hour, they kept moving without a rest. Deborah, marching among the men, suddenly realized what she had done. She felt terror. If the army found out she was a woman, she surely would be punished. She might be hanged!

Deborah calmed herself. In the days and months ahead, she would have to be watchful. She would play the part of a quiet young man who kept to himself.

After ten tiring days, the recruits reached West Point in New York. There, they received uniforms and weapons. Deborah began training as a foot soldier in the Fourth Massachusetts Regiment.

The war was winding down. But British troops and Tory bands were still active in New York. Deborah joined scouting parties hunting for armed Tories. She faced musket fire. She heard the cries of the wounded. She saw men fall beside her. Luckily, she escaped unharmed.

Then came a morning when Deborah was not so lucky. In a battle with Tories, she was wounded in the head and leg. She begged her comrades not to take her to the hospital. "Let me die here," she pleaded. But they did not listen.

A French doctor at a field hospital treated Deborah's head. She said she had no other wound. The doctor noticed the bloody boot. "Sit you down, my lad," said the doctor, preparing to look at the leg. But Deborah said there was no need.

She secretly tried to remove the musket ball from her own thigh, with no success. The wound would heal, but not fully.

In 1783, Deborah was among the troops in Philadelphia. Sickness spread throughout the city. She became ill. She was brought to a hospital. Her fever was so high that she passed out. When a doctor looked her over, he discovered that the soldier called Robert Shurtlieff was really a girl.

Soon afterward, Deborah Sampson received an honorable discharge from the Continental Army. She returned to Massachusetts.

Deborah Sampson married a farmer named Benjamin Gannett. The couple had three children. They struggled to make a living on their farm.

Years later, Deborah Gannett met a newspaper publisher. He wrote a book based on her life.

The Gannetts worked hard. But they still owed money. In 1802, the newspaper publisher came to Deborah with another idea. How would she like to make money by telling her story to audiences?

In 1802, women did not go on speaking tours. It just was not done. Deborah Sampson Gannett, forty-two years old, thought about the newspaperman's offer. She would have to travel from city to city on her own. She would have to perform before strangers. She would have to memorize a fifteen-page speech.

Deborah said yes. She would do it.

AN

A D D R

DELIVERED WITH AP

AT THE *FEDERAL STREET THEATRE,*
FOUR SUCCESSIVE NIGHTS OF THE DIFFERENT
PLAYS, BEGINNING *MARCH 21, 1893*

AND AFTER, AT OTHER PRINCIPAL TOWNS, A
NUMBER OF NIGHTS SUCCESSIVELY
AT EACH PLACE;

BY MRS. DEBORAH GANNETT

THE AMERICAN HEROINE.

Who served three years with reputation (undiscovered as a
Female) in the late AMERICAN ARMY.

———————

Audiences paid to see the unusual soldier. In uniform, Deborah Sampson Gannett performed the drills she had learned as Private Shurtlieff.

She gave her speech in a confident voice. Pretending to be a man was a "bad deed," she admitted. She had taken steps that women were not permitted to take. Terrible memories of the "storms of war" would always be with her. Yet she had done it for the best reasons — liberty and independence.

The new United States government granted small monthly payments to those who had served in the war. Deborah Sampson Gannett was granted payments for her faithful service as a soldier of the Revolution.

Responding

Think About the Story

1. What is the first unfortunate thing to happen to Deborah?

2. What things make it possible for Deborah to pretend to be Robert Shurtlieff?

3. Pretend you are Mrs. Thomas. Make a numbered list of directions for Deborah Sampson to follow when she completes her jobs on the farm. Begin with **1. Get up at dawn.**

Following Directions

Help Deborah Sampson plan her speech. Write these directions in the right order on a piece of paper. Circle the clue words.

Third, tell about the hardships of army life.
Next, tell about being a bound girl.
Finally, tell about how you were wounded.
First, begin with your early life.